God's Answer for You

God's Answer for You

Psalms That Speak to Real-life Needs

Bruce L. Petersen

Beacon Hill Press of Kansas City
Kansas City, Missouri

Copyright 1994
by Beacon Hill Press of Kansas City

ISBN: 083-411-4933

Printed in the
United States of America

Cover Design: Royce Ratcliff

10   9   8   7   6   5   4   3   2   1

To my wife, friend, and companion, Jackie,
for her encouragement and support for this project.
She generously granted me hours and days for work
that could have been spent with her.
She has also been a wonderful mother
to our children—Heather and Erik.

Contents

Contents

Acknowledgments

Let me express my deep gratitude:

To College Church of the Nazarene in Nampa, Idaho, the church I am privileged to pastor. They listened with patience and enthusiasm as these concepts were preached from the pulpit in sermon form.

To Dr. Percival and Marjorie Wesche for making available a lovely cottage in the mountains of Idaho each year for study and writing. Creative thoughts flow easily in such a beautiful setting.

To my sister-in-law Sally Petersen for her professional editorial help in smoothing out the rough edges of this manuscript. Her encouragement and suggestions helped me finally finish.

To Jan McNaught and Clara Watts for reading the manuscript and offering helpful improvements to the text.

To God be the glory!

Introduction

"You don't understand!" It's a pet phrase teenagers use when they talk to their parents. Each generation has the idea the issues they deal with have never before confronted mankind.

There *is* a sense in which each generation faces new challenges, however. Napoleon never wondered how he could use his air force at the Battle of Waterloo—airplanes had not yet been invented. And imagine Abraham Lincoln having his Gettysburg Address beamed around the world by satellite. People alive today have seen more changes in communication, transportation, and medicine than any other generation in history.

Yet when it comes to the inner issues of life, things haven't changed a whole lot since the beginning of time. Problems such as guilt, fear, and depression have plagued mankind since Adam and Eve were driven from the Garden of Eden.

This is why the book we call Psalms has become one of the best-loved portions of the Bible. Although many of these songs from the Jewish hymnbook are more than 3,000 years old, they deal with issues that have affected people of every generation—up to the present one. Written by various poets over centuries of time, these verses were inspired by God to remind His people how these basic issues could be faced and conquered.

For this book I have selected psalms that show God's instructions for facing the following issues: direction for life, inferiority, discouragement, unjust treatment, fear, guilt, worry, depression, and stress. These are the issues that move the best-sellers at your local bookstore. These are the subjects discussed on the popular television talk shows.

Isn't it time we realize that God understands these basic issues in our lives—and take time to discover the answers He has for us?

1

God's Answer for Your Need of Direction

Blessed is the man who does not walk in the counsel of the wicked or stand in the way of sinners or sit in the seat of mockers. But his delight is in the law of the Lord, and on his law he meditates day and night. He is like a tree planted by streams of water, which yields its fruit in season and whose leaf does not wither. Whatever he does prospers.

Not so the wicked! They are like chaff that the wind blows away. Therefore the wicked will not stand in the judgment, nor sinners in the assembly of the righteous.

For the Lord watches over the way of the righteous, but the way of the wicked will perish.

—Psalm 1

Choices—life is made up of them. Some are easily made because they carry little consequence. The choice between vanilla and chocolate ice cream is not a weighty one. Other choices are more difficult because they have the power to alter the course of life.

Robert Frost's familiar poem "The Road Not Taken" reminds us of the impact choices have on our lives. Frost takes us on a walk on a wooded road that forks into two trails. Both look equally inviting, but the hiker must make a choice. He concludes his verse with an observation about life's choices:

> *And both that morning equally lay*
> *In leaves no step had trodden black.*
> *Oh, I kept the first for another day!*
> *Yet knowing how way leads on to way,*
> *I doubted if I should ever come back.*
>
> *I shall be telling this with a sigh*
> *Somewhere ages and ages hence:*
> *Two roads diverged in a wood, and I—*
> *I took the one less traveled by,*
> *And that has made all the difference.*[1]

If we reduce life to its simplest terms, there is one choice that outranks all others. That choice is the direction our lives will follow. The Psalmist says there are only two roads through life. We will all make a choice to walk one of those ways. Psalm 1 contrasts the two ways and their ultimate destinations.

GO GOD'S WAY

Going God's way results in a happy life. The Psalmist begins this poem with the word **blessed,** which in the Hebrew means "happy" or "joyous." It comes from a verb that means "to go forth, advance, or lead the way." God intends for Christians to be leading the way, setting the pace with a joyous attitude.

Here's an interesting paradox: People who seek happiness for its own sake will not find it. It's like trying to capture moonbeams in a jar. However, those who seek God will discover happiness as a serendipity.

Have you purchased a new appliance recently? Every manufacturer inserts an instruction manual with the product. Its purpose is clear—to help you use the machine as the inventor intended. While many of those instruction books are nearly impossible to understand, God's plan for us is amazingly simple: He created us to walk with Him in fellowship. Is it any wonder that real satisfaction and joy come only as we walk His way?

Going God's way means we must choose to do right. The Bible is very straightforward: don't **walk in the counsel of the wicked** (v. 1). We can no longer be willing participants in sin. This calls for a conscious decision to turn away from the old way so that we can walk with Christ. Prov. 4:14 restates the truth: **Do not set foot on the path of the wicked or** *walk in the way* **of evil men** (emphasis added).

Going God's way means following the truth. For the Psalmist, there is only one truth—the **law of the Lord** (v. 2). In his day the law was the Law of Moses. It gave a limited picture of God's plan for mankind. Now, knowing the truth is not a problem. The Bible gives a clear picture of what God wants us to know.

Choosing to do right and following the truth are not enough. Do we have the right attitude? The Psalmist encourages us to **delight . . . in the law of the Lord** (v. 2). How do we view the Bible? Is it a restriction, something that keeps us from doing what we want? God's law is far more. It's a game plan for effective living.

Imagine a football game without rules. Every player could do as he pleased. Who would determine what was out-of-bounds? What would be the criteria for scoring a touchdown? Without the benefit of rules, the stadium would empty in five minutes. Why? Rules and boundaries give the game of football meaning. When we **delight,** we accept God's game plan, not chafing under its limitations.

In verse 2 the Psalmist moves us from right attitudes to right actions: **On his law he meditates day and night.** Picture a cow ruminating or chewing her cud. She chews over and over on the grass earlier consumed to get maximum benefit from the food. This doesn't sound very appetizing, does it? Yet this is exactly what we do mentally when we **meditate.** We become so immersed in the Word that we dwell upon it. We mull it over in our minds constantly until it becomes a part of our lives.

15

Going God's way means developing the right life. Verse 3 compares the Christian life to a tree. The implications for us as believers are rich.

Remain planted—**by streams of water** (v. 3). The roots provide an anchor from the storms as well as a pipeline for the nutrients in the ground to feed the whole plant. I recently pulled a weed from my small garden. To my surprise, the root was nearly as long as the plant above ground. It was firmly planted.

Be productive—**yields its fruit in season** (v. 3). Jesus had very little tolerance for the fig tree with lots of leaves but no fruit. As you draw from the life-giving flow of the Spirit, you should naturally produce a harvest of spiritual fruit. Don't be afraid to ask yourself, "Where's the fruit?"

Live a potent life—**whose leaf does not wither** (v. 3). One of the scenes I enjoyed when I lived in the Midwest was the beautiful fall foliage. My wife and I took many drives to see the spectacular display of God's handiwork. However lovely, colored leaves are not a sign of life, but death. They will soon be decaying on the ground. Green leaves show that the tree is still vigorous.

Enjoy a prosperous life—**whatever he does prospers** (v. 3). This prosperity theology has nothing to do with financial gain. It is a soul prosperity. The Father wants us to enjoy the benefits that come from being a part of His "forever family."

About this time you may be asking if this is for real. Can a person really experience life like this? One thing is for certain: real living does not come by simply trying harder or starting over. How can we choose to do right, follow the truth, and develop the right life? Look no further than Jesus Christ. He made this statement about himself: **I am the way and the truth and the life** (John 14:6).

John Wesley came face-to-face with a robber one night on a lonely road. The highwayman voiced his disappointment when he received only a few coins. Wesley said to the man, "If you ever want to change, remember: the blood of

Jesus Christ, God's Son, cleanseth from all sin." Years later this same man identified himself to Wesley at the end of a service. No longer a thief, he was a well-to-do tradesman. With a deep sense of gratitude the man said, "To you, dear sir, I owe it all." Wesley replied, "No, not to me, but to the blood of Jesus, which cleanses."

ABANDON YOUR OWN WAY

It is easy to label wicked people as those who spend time in jail for murder, theft, or rape. Yet the **wicked** person mentioned in verse 4 is anyone who has chosen to neglect God. Such a person lives life on the horizontal plane with no regard for the vertical dimension.

A minister friend of mine and I were once teamed up on the golf course with a very pleasant, middle-aged couple. As we walked the fairways, they discovered that we were ministers. The wife felt she needed to respond in some way, so she said, "We have never attended church. We never felt we ever really needed it."

The writer of Proverbs provides an interesting response: **There is a way that seems right to a man, but in the end it leads to death** (14:12).

A self-centered life does not finish well. The two words **not so** (v. 4) sum it up well. Everything you can say about the righteous man is **not so** for **the wicked.**

Are you traveling your own way? If so, you are standing **in the way of sinners** (v. 1). And if we stand in the sinner's highway, eventually we'll be traveling with them.

Are you hearing the truth? It is so easy to listen to the **counsel of the wicked** (v. 1). There are so many voices giving advice and exerting influence. It's hard to know whom to follow. We may be taking our cues from ungodly work associates, peers at school, or the secular media. Ralph Waldo Emerson was right: "Truth is beautiful, without doubt, but so are lies."

Have you found the right life? Do you spend your days sitting **in the seat of mockers** (v. 1)? Who are the patternmakers of your life? For many today, the models are the rock stars, professional athletes, or successful media people. To **sit in the seat of mockers** means we want to experience their lives. We want to be just like them. But if we could look beneath the glamorous exterior, we might discover deep unhappiness. Consider the many who find themselves in treatment centers for alcohol and drug addictions.

The problem with a self-centered life is its shallowness. The Psalmist describes it **like chaff that the wind blows away** (v. 4). Chaff is like fluff. It has no stability. It simply follows the wind. Chaff has no lasting value. The winnowers toss it in the air to separate it from the valuable wheat. What is it in life that has permanent, lasting value for you? Stocks can lose their value overnight. A house can burn to the ground. Degrees and honors are quickly forgotten.

Jesus told a parable of a rich farmer who thought he was building security through barns and crops. God's response was **You fool! This very night your life will be demanded from you. Then who will get what you have prepared for yourself?** Jesus then gave this summary: **This is how it will be with anyone who stores up things for himself but is not rich toward God** (Luke 12:20, 21).

A self-centered life does not offer much for the future. The Psalmist says it **will not stand in the judgment** (v. 5). Selfishness cannot withstand the scrutiny of a holy God who will be the righteous Judge.

CHOOSING THE BEST

Does it pay to walk with God? Of course! He offers a bright present and a promising future. **For the Lord watches over the way of the righteous** (v. 6). It's not simply that He is watching down from heaven. The Hebrew word translated as **watches over** refers to the intimate way God knows us. Each moment, He knows exactly where we are on the journey. We can walk with Him.

TAKE ACTION

1. Take a moment to chart what the destination of your life will be if you continue on your present course. It may be time for some midcourse corrections. The longer you go without adjustment, the harder it is to change.

2. Imagine Jesus walking right beside you. See how His presence affects the way you think and act. Picture Him giving you courage to make difficult choices. Sense Him directing you at those forks in the road.

Jesus, thank You for giving me direction and accompanying me on the journey.

2

God's Answer for Your Feelings of Inferiority

O Lord, our Lord, how majestic is your name in all the earth!

You have set your glory above the heavens. From the lips of children and infants you have ordained praise because of your enemies, to silence the foe and the avenger.

When I consider your heavens, the work of your fingers, the moon and the stars, which you have set in place, what is man that you are mindful of him, the son of man that you care for him? You made him a little lower than the heavenly beings and crowned him with glory and honor.

You made him ruler over the works of your hands; you put everything under his feet: all flocks and herds, and the beasts of the field, the birds of the air, and the fish of the sea, all that swim the paths of the seas.

O Lord, our Lord, how majestic is your name in all the earth!

—Psalm 8

What is man? That question has been asked ever since Adam and Eve first walked out of the garden to face an unfriendly world. It's a question we ask at the birth of a baby. It's on the mind of those who peer into the casket of

20

a loved one. As the world mourns the loss of countless lives at the end of a war, the same question is asked: What is man?

Charles Darwin promoted the theory that man is nothing more than an advanced animal, with little to make him unique from the rest of the animal kingdom. Karl Marx believed that man is just an economic factor whose only value is to build a classless society. Well-known astronomer Carl Sagan said, "As long as there have been humans, we have searched for our place in the cosmos. Where are we? Who are we? We find that we live on an insignificant planet of a humdrum star lost in a galaxy tucked away on some forgotten corner of a universe in which there are far more galaxies than people." Without a caring God, man simply shrivels into insignificance in this vast universe.

Imagine David, the shepherd boy, watching sheep and staring into the starlit sky. He muses over the basic question regarding his existence: What is man?

This question plagues all our thoughts as we face life. It's easy to think, If I am nothing more than an advanced animal, then why shouldn't I go ahead and satisfy my basic animal urges? If I am nothing more than an economic factor, then why not try to grab all the marbles I can before the game is over? But then, if I am nothing more than a little grease spot in the corner of the universe, why bother living at all?

Our value is not determined by what others think of us, however. It's not even what we think of ourselves. The only one that can really determine our worth is the one who created us, God himself. In Psalm 8 God gives four reasons He thinks we are important.

GOD SAYS: "YOU ARE IMPORTANT BECAUSE I MADE YOU"

It's nice to know where we stand in the divine pecking order. David says, **You made him a little lower than the heavenly beings** (v. 5). The word translated **heavenly be-**

21

ings is *elohim,* the plural word for God himself. Think of it! In God's eyes, our significance is just beneath the Trinity.

This verse reminds us that we are unique creations of God. You and I are not the result of some cosmic accident. We are more like our Creator than anything He made. In the Genesis account of creation God said, **Let us make man in our image, in our likeness** (1:26). Why? So that the invisible God could become visible in creation. This means that everyone, even the Hitlers and Stalins of our world, has a trace of the image of God, distorted though it may be. Of course, the image has been perfectly reflected to us through the Son, Jesus Christ.

Each individual is significant. As gospel singer Ethel Waters used to say, "God made me, and God don't make no junk."

GOD SAYS: "YOU ARE IMPORTANT BECAUSE I WATCH OVER YOU"

Sometimes we forget just how vast this universe is and that God is in control of all of it. When David stared off into the clear night sky, he could see only a few thousand stars. Today, with modern telescopes, we can see a billion stars. Even so, he was filled with awe.

Scientists believe that within the universe may be a hundred billion galaxies, each with a hundred billion stars. Suffice it to say, we just can't comprehend how big the universe really is.

It's easy to feel insignificant if we think of ourselves as only specks on a tiny planet over in the corner of space. But God doesn't measure significance by size. In the vastness of His creation, God is **mindful** (v. 4) of every one of us. Like David, we can't understand how or why, but it's true. In Matthew and Luke, Jesus reminds us that if God considers a tiny sparrow, He certainly cares much more about us. Nothing we do or say escapes His awareness and concern.

Not long ago, I traveled by plane via Chicago. On this particular day O'Hare Field certainly lived up to its reputation as the busiest airport in the world. I was reminded of the man who told the ticket agent he wanted to fly from Chicago to New York by way of San Francisco, Dallas, and Atlanta. When the agent behind the counter asked why, the man replied, "That's the way my luggage went the last time I made this flight."

We're used to mixups and impersonal treatment in our crowded world—but not from God. He knows every person who walks through O'Hare—each person's dreams, joys, and heartaches. It's the same for all people throughout the world. Most important, He knows you.

GOD SAYS: "YOU ARE IMPORTANT BECAUSE I VALUE YOU"

David assures us in verse 5 that God has crowned us **with glory and honor.** God has gifted us with His own attributes. **Glory** means value and potential, while **honor** signifies the recognition of status and position.

Everyone likes to know exactly where he ranks in comparison to other people. While we may have our own ideas about our importance, when someone we respect tells us we are valued, we tend to believe it more.

God says He created us **a little lower than the heavenly beings** or, as it can also be translated, **than God** (margin). There is nothing God has made that is any more important to Him than you are.

God did more than merely talk about our worth to Him. He proved His esteem for us through action. Jesus' birth, death, and resurrection were tangible demonstrations of His great love for us.

Many years ago, an Englishman was taken captive by a group of Abyssinians. They threw him into a dungeon in the city of Magdala. When the English government found out that one of their citizens had been captured, they demanded his instant release. The captors refused the request. Enraged, the British sent an armada of ships with many troops who stormed the dungeon and freed the Eng-

23

lishman. Later, while counting the cost of this rescue, the government discovered it had spent $25 million to free one man. The man must have felt himself quite valuable to have warranted such an expensive rescue.[2]

God paid a much higher price to rescue us from the clutches of Satan. Money alone would not have done the job. God gave what was closest to His own heart to set us free—His only Son, Jesus. We need but to look at the Cross to understand how much God values us.

GOD SAYS: "YOU ARE IMPORTANT BECAUSE I COMMISSION YOU"

Just as God has dominion over the universe, verses 6-8 tell us He has given man rulership over the earth.

One of the earliest commands of God to Adam and Eve in the garden was **Be fruitful and increase in number; fill the earth and subdue it** (Gen. 1:28). This is one of the few commands we have fulfilled. The earth is certainly filled, almost to overflowing in some places.

We haven't followed through with the second part of God's admonition. Instead of subduing the earth, we have destroyed many of the things over which God has given us authority. Our air and water, both necessary for life, are becoming increasingly polluted. The ravaging of our natural resources speaks of a callous disregard for future generations.

Most tragic of all is that in our attempts to subdue the earth, we have been unable to subdue *ourselves*. In searching for the enemy, we have discovered that he is us. Lurking deep within, sometimes cleverly camouflaged, is the culprit: sin. Violence, greed, and perversion are the results, and we can see them all around us. Sin has distorted our value system.

You and I can only begin to understand our true worth as we are in a right relationship with God. But when David asked: **What is man . . . ?** he asked it of the One who has the answer.

God answers that important question by introducing us to the ideal Man, Jesus, the Second Adam in the flesh. The writer of Hebrews must have been thinking of this in 2:9—**But we see Jesus, who was made a little lower than the angels, now crowned with glory and honor because he suffered death, so that by the grace of God he might taste death for everyone.**

The road to true self-worth begins when we receive Jesus into our lives. In Christ we find our value, our purpose, and our hope.

WHO AM I?

You may be wrestling with an image of yourself shaped by painful failures of the past. You may have painted your self-portrait based on shortcomings and cruel things others have said or done to you. Do you want the real truth? You are someone very special to God, because you are His special creation. And no matter what you've done, how you've failed, or how others have affected you, through Jesus Christ you can be what you were created to be.

TAKE ACTION

1. Read again the account in John 4:1-29 of Jesus' compassion to the woman at the well. Instead of condemning her for her unsavory past, He offered her hope of a new life. Jesus values you in the same way. By faith, accept His love.

2. Affirm a family member or friend who is battling feelings of low self-worth. Your valuing that person may be God's way of expressing His love.

Father, thank You for creating me, loving me, and adopting me as Your child.

3

God's Answer for Your Discouragement

How long, O Lord? Will you forget me forever? How long will you hide your face from me? How long must I wrestle with my thoughts and every day have sorrow in my heart? How long will my enemy triumph over me?

Look on me and answer, O Lord my God. Give light to my eyes, or I will sleep in death; my enemy will say, "I have overcome him," and my foes will rejoice when I fall.

But I trust in your unfailing love; my heart rejoices in your salvation. I will sing to the Lord, for he has been good to me.

—Psalm 13

A novelist tells about a severe famine that struck Ireland. To help provide for the starving peasants, jobs were created so that money could be earned in an honorable way. Men were given hand tools with which to begin the construction of a new road. The workers whistled and sang as they labored. Later they discovered that the road they were building ended in a swamp. With that realization, a change came over the workers. Cheerfulness disappeared. A mood of anger and unhappiness prevailed. The observation was made that "roads that lead nowhere are hard to build."[3]

David knew that feeling. He had been a real-life national hero. Against great odds he had single-handedly defeated Goliath, the nation's public enemy number one. Despite David's victories, King Saul was not cheering this young champion. Saul saw David as a threat to his leadership; and as a result David had to flee for his life. Just when it seemed that life was falling into place for David, it took a sharp turn for the worse. Once a hero, he was now a fugitive.

How should we respond when it seems as though life plays its cruel tricks on us? David confronts the subject of tough times by revealing in Psalm 13 three different responses we can take when discouragement comes.

1. WE CAN LOOK AT OURSELVES IN PITY

David's first response to trouble in verses 1 and 2 is a familiar one to many of us. He was overwhelmed by the problem and cried out four times: **How long?**

Have you ever felt the weight of discouragement so heavy upon your shoulders that all you could do is heave a sigh? Instead of saying, "How long?" you might sigh and ask, "Why me? Why now? Why so severe?"

When we are discouraged, we can certainly identify with David's continuing complaint: **Will you forget me forever?** It's easy to be discouraged when we think we are abandoned. But will an omniscient God forget us for even one moment, let alone forever? Isaiah reminds us, **Can a mother forget the baby at her breast and have no compassion on the child she has borne? Though she may forget, I will not forget you!** (49:15).

We may also be tempted to say, "God is ignoring me. Maybe God does know who I am, but is He hiding from me?" Our egos are damaged when we feel ignored by the significant people in our lives.

In self-pity we may cry out, "I am hurting inside." David asked the question, **How long must I wrestle with my thoughts and every day have sorrow in my heart?** (v.

2). In the face of discouraging situations, we may feel we are facing the battle alone. Somehow, the emotional strength just isn't there.

If that weren't enough, David asks, **How long will my enemy triumph over me?** (v. 2). In other words, "How much more of this humiliation can I stand?" How do we feel when people seem to take special delight in stomping our good name into the ground? I know what happens to me. I usually finish the job the gossipers began by doubting myself. But self-pity is not the solution to discouragement.

2. WE CAN LONG FOR GOD IN PRAYER

When we are discouraged, our emotions can reach avalanche proportions. We begin to feel that if we don't talk to someone, we'll burst. David felt that way too. After overcoming his feelings of self-pity, he called out to God.

If we were following David's prayer, we might cry out, "Lord, if You're out there, let me know." David shouted out this attention-getter: **Look on me** (v. 3). He wanted God to give him some attention.

When our daughter, Heather, was about three years old, she was very interested in having my full attention when she was talking. If I wasn't listening, she would crawl up on my lap, place her hands on my face, and turn my head until I was looking directly into her eyes. That's what David was trying to do with God.

Why doesn't God respond immediately when we call? That's a question that has long plagued believers. The answer, I suspect, has to do with the strengthening of our faith. The first Russian cosmonaut who returned from a long-term space voyage experienced real adjustment difficulties from the 211 days of weightlessness. He was dizzy, couldn't walk, and suffered atrophied muscles. Why? The body in zero gravity needs little exertion to function, because there is no resistance. To overcome this problem on future flights, scientists developed a "penguin suit" with elastic bands that would resist every move. Even in zero gravity, the cosmonaut would have to exert muscle strength to make any move. Without God allowing us to face difficulties, we would never build faith.

When he was discouraged, David prayed this way: **Give light to my eyes** (v. 3). "Help me see the big picture." When discouragement comes, it is easy to develop a case of spiritual myopia. Instead, we can pray, "Lord, help me see the truth."

In 2 Kings 6 we find a great story involving the prophet Elisha. The armies of the enemy country, Aram, had surrounded the prophet and his servant. The servant was discouraged because the odds seemed so enormously against them. Beginning in verse 16, we read Elisha's words: **Don't be afraid . . . Those who are with us are more than those who are with them.** Then he prayed, **O Lord, open his eyes so he may see.** When the servant looked up, he suddenly saw the hills full of horses and chariots of fire.

Is it possible to come to the point in prayer at which we say, "Lord, I release my problem to You"? Consider David's response to the enemy's attacks in verse 4—"So what!" We can learn to say the same thing. It doesn't matter what our enemy says or does. God can handle our problems better than we can. With a sigh of relief, we can release everything to a God who never ignores us. He's there, and that's enough.

3. WE CAN LIFT OUR PRAISE TO GOD

With God's help, we can be overcomers. We don't need to stay in the pits. Victory comes as we make the proper faith responses.

One such response is *trust.* **I trust in your unfailing love** (v. 5). The object of our trust is all-important. We've all tried to operate on our own and failed enough times to know that self-sufficiency doesn't work.

The words of the familiar hymn "Stand Up for Jesus" remind us: "The arm of flesh will fail you— / Ye dare not trust your own." Is your confidence in the steadfast, faithful love of a God who does what is best?

Young John Fletcher was interested in traveling from England to the New World during the days when ships were the only option. He contacted a sailing captain and made arrangements to make the voyage with the crew. On the day before the trip, John was scalded on the leg as his servant attempted to serve him tea. The burns were so severe that the ship's captain refused to allow young Fletcher on board for the trip. John was very disappointed. However, it later proved that God was actually acting in love for young John. It turned out that those who watched that ship sail from England were the last ever to see the vessel.[4]

Another faith response is *praise*. David makes this strong assertion: **My heart rejoices in your salvation** (v. 5). It's hard for me to rejoice when I am discouraged. But it can be done when I recognize that even the worst of my problems are temporary. Salvation is for eternity, and that's exciting!

Singing can be part of our praise offering to God. David had long ago discovered the soothing effect of the harp and voice upon the soul. Singing is active praise to our God. It is also a testimony to others and a powerful declaration to Satan. Martin Luther, who was well-known for his hymn writing, once said, "The devil . . . cannot endure sacred songs of joy. Our passions and impatiences, . . . and our Woe is Me! please the devil well; but our songs and psalms vex him and grieve him sorely."[5]

A third faith response is *thanks*. David's final statement of appreciation says it all: **He has been good to me** (v. 6). Notice that David speaks in the past perfect tense. We have a history to call upon—God's grace to us is and has always been beyond our expectation. As we reflect on His goodness in the past, the discouragements of the present are not that big after all.

God uses the discouraging times to shape us. An old Chinese proverb says it this way: "A gem cannot be pol-

ished without friction, nor a man perfected without trials."
We can allow discouragement to defeat us, or to motivate
us to rise to victory over it with God's help. Our response
makes all the difference.

TAKE ACTION

1. Take a good look at whatever is discouraging you. Do
you have any control over the situation? If you can't
change it, give it to God.

2. Pay a visit to someone who is discouraged. A plate of
cookies or a thoughtful card may turn the person's vision
heavenward.

*Father, help me look beyond my trials to see Your hand at work
in my life. You can help me know victory as You perfect me for
Your glory. Amen.*

4

God's Answer for Facing Unjust Treatment

Vindicate me, O Lord, for I have led a blameless life; I have trusted in the Lord without wavering. Test me, O Lord, and try me, examine my heart and my mind; for your love is ever before me, and I walk continually in your truth. I do not sit with deceitful men, nor do I consort with hypocrites; I abhor the assembly of evildoers and refuse to sit with the wicked. I wash my hands in innocence, and go about your altar, O Lord, proclaiming aloud your praise and telling of all your wonderful deeds. I love the house where you live, O Lord, the place where your glory dwells.

Do not take away my soul along with sinners, my life with bloodthirsty men, in whose hands are wicked schemes, whose right hands are full of bribes. But I lead a blameless life; redeem me and be merciful to me.

My feet stand on level ground; in the great assembly I will praise the Lord.

—Psalm 26

A man in a church I once pastored developed a strong dislike for me as a pastor. I don't know why he found my pastoral style or personal skills so distasteful. Talking to him about the problem never provided a satisfactory answer. I went overboard at times to win him over by being friendly, but even that was misinterpreted. Even today I have an uncomfortable feeling when I think about my failure to establish good rapport with him.

We all like to be accepted, understood, and appreciated. The way others view us affects our self-esteem. Most of us have known people who have misunderstood our motives and misinterpreted our actions. We are hurt when our basic character has been attacked. "Why doesn't this person understand who I really am?" we ask.

We have already seen that David understood what it meant to be treated unjustly. He had bravely fought and defeated Goliath to defend Israel's honor. In the aftermath of the Philistine defeat, David became a national hero. As the victorious army marched through the towns of Israel, the women danced and sang, **Saul has slain his thousands, and David his tens of thousands** (1 Sam. 18:7). The next day an evil spirit of jealousy came over King Saul. While David was playing his harp for the king, Saul hurled a spear at David, trying to pin him to the wall. This was the first of several times that Saul attempted to take David's life.

Can you imagine David's feelings of hurt and confusion? Saul's angry attack was unfair; he had meant the king no harm. In fact, all of David's efforts were motivated by love and loyalty to Saul. To be treated with jealousy and contempt was a real slap in the face. It may be that David wrote Psalm 26 as he struggled to recover from the unjust treatment at Saul's hands.

What can you and I do when we are treated unfairly? Is there a better answer than to strike back in revenge? How can we keep from being totally devastated by the attack? Psalm 26 offers four steps we can take when we are unjustly treated.

STEP ONE: TEST YOUR MOTIVES

When you and I are attacked, we have a tendency to become defensive. We want to justify our actions. If only they could understand my motives, we think, they would know I meant no harm.

Jesus addressed this issue in the Sermon on the Mount when He talked about being slapped on the right cheek. For a right-handed person to slap someone else on the right cheek would take a backhanded blow. It's the epitome of an insult if you are on the receiving end. Your honor may be at stake, and your first response probably is to double your fist and strike out in anger. Yet Jesus suggests, **If someone strikes you on the right cheek, turn to him the other also** (Matt. 5:39).

But how can I keep from reacting first and thinking later? David asked God for a thorough, objective appraisal of his motives. **Test me, O Lord, and try me, examine my heart and my mind** (v. 2). David was serious about wanting God's input. He asked God to **test . . . try . . . examine**. The word translated **examine** means to refine gold by heating it to a molten consistency and skimming off the impurities. If I ask God to **examine** me, I am making myself vulnerable to a complete scrutiny of my inner motivations. He has the right to expose not only my faults but also my feeble attempts to rationalize them.

After the Holy Spirit exposes those secret faults in my life, I must be willing to allow them to be placed in God's refining fire. The end result is the perfecting of my character. God can use painful, unjust treatment as a means of spiritual development.

How can we be sure our motives are pure and not self-centered? David gives us the answer in verse 3: **For your love is ever before me, and I walk continually in your truth.** Knowing that God loves us unconditionally helps us realize that He is the only One we need to please. His truth, as revealed in Scripture, is the objective yardstick we need in order to keep our motives pure. God has a way of gently personalizing His truth to each person's situation so that our heart's desire is right toward God and our fellowman.

STEP TWO: TURN FROM NEGATIVE INFLUENCES

When we have been wronged, our natural tendency is to find someone to tell. A true friend can listen, support, and give advice. However, David warns against telling our woes to the wrong people: **I do not sit with deceitful men ... hypocrites ... evildoers ... the wicked"** (vv. 4-5).

Wrong influencers can encourage self-pity. We can always find someone who will hear our story and say, "Poor baby!" That person will tell us what we want to hear, not what we need to hear. A piece of sage advice comes from Prov. 27:6—**Wounds from a friend can be trusted, but an enemy multiplies kisses.**

Wrong influencers often encourage revenge. You have been wronged, they say. You have been hurt. It is only fair that your enemy suffer. Besides, just think how good you will feel when you see them hurting. Revenge is the only way to right the wrong.

While I was pastoring in Saginaw, Mich., a feud broke out between two large families in the city. A young man from one family was killed by members of the other family. The mourning family felt duty-bound to avenge the death by killing a member of the enemy family. The second family then retaliated for the death they had suffered. Back and forth the two families fought. Several payback deaths pained both families before a priest was able to negotiate peace.

The assumption that getting even will settle the score is false. It never does. Revenge is never sweet. Instead, we should follow Paul's directive: **Do not repay anyone evil for evil. Be careful to do what is right in the eyes of everybody. If it is possible, as far as it depends on you, live at peace with everyone. Do not take revenge, my friends, but leave room for God's wrath, for it is written: "It is mine to avenge; I will repay," says the Lord** (Rom. 12:17-19).

STEP THREE: TRUST IN GOD

David knew that God would understand his situation, so he went to the Tabernacle. **I love the house where you live, O Lord, the place where your glory dwells** (v. 8). What happens when we turn to God after we've been wronged?

God's love gives us confidence to try again. David felt it—**for your love is ever before me** (v. 3). What a comfort to know that God's love is there all the time! A single friend once asked a father of four, "Why do you love your kids?" The father thought for a moment and then answered, "Because they're mine." What a joy to know that as God's child, I receive His personal love and attention.

With God's sense of justice, right will eventually prevail. David began his prayer, **Vindicate me, O Lord, for I have led a blameless life** (v. 1). **Vindicate** means to clear from criticism, to defend, to justify. David wanted God to tell the world he was innocent. In our lives that doesn't always happen. There are people that will never know, or may choose not to believe, the real truth about us.

But God has the ability to see into our innermost motivation. He knows our hearts when others don't understand. He has a way of righting wrongs in His own time. Knowing that God is going to handle our situation relieves the pressure of feeling we have to handle it ourselves.

Like David, you can find strength through public worship. Even though David was under fire, he found delight in being in the house of the Lord. Worship can provide rest, retreat, and renewal. You can leave a gathering of God's family with a new resolve to face your foes.

STEP FOUR: TAKE THE HIGH ROAD

While others may consider underhanded deception, David made a commitment to integrity. **But I lead a blameless life** (v. 11). "Let others sink to cruel and unethical behavior; not me!" David declares.

The high road of personal integrity is not always easy to travel. People will not always understand your refusal to get even.

My friend Jack (not his real name) was in a partnership that had to declare bankruptcy because of the poor judgment of the partner. My friend was accused, even though he was personally innocent of any wrongdoing. While the partner hid behind loopholes in the law, Jack personally paid back all the debts of his partner. While it took Jack years to reimburse all the creditors, God richly blessed him for taking the high road.

God also encourages us to take a long view of life. David concludes his petition to God by declaring, **My feet stand on level ground** (v. 12). He was taking a stance where he could gain a better perspective.

I am writing these words from a cabin high in the mountains of Idaho. From my vantage point, all I can see in any direction are tall pine trees. My clear vision is limited to 100 yards at best. Where I live down in a broad valley in Idaho, I can see for 30 or 40 miles in any direction on a clear day.

When confronted with unjust treatment, I can choose to focus my attention on my surroundings in the here and now. Like towering trees, the issues may seem completely over my head. But I can choose to make my stance on level ground. From there, I can see that this momentary difficulty may be of little importance when placed in eternal perspective.

WE SHALL OVERCOME

Life isn't fair. Injustices happen. People can be cruel. The question is—What are you going to do about unjust treatment when it hits you personally? God will help you if you are willing to (1) test your motives, (2) turn from negative influences, (3) trust in God, and (4) take the high road. You can be an overcomer.

TAKE ACTION

1. Choose now whether you will be a victim or a victor when you are wrongly treated. Victims lie down in self-pity. Victors try everything they know to overcome.

2. Rather than ignoring those who have hurt you, pray for them. Jesus says, **Love your enemies and pray for those who persecute you** (Matt. 5:44). As you show concern for them, you may discover that they have been misunderstood also.

Father, when my enemies mistreat me, may I follow Jesus' example on the Cross by praying, "Father, forgive them."

5

God's Answer
for Your Fear

*The Lord is my light and my salvation—whom shall I fear?
The Lord is the stronghold of my life—of whom shall I be afraid?
When evil men advance against me to devour my flesh, when my
enemies and my foes attack me, they will stumble and fall.
Though an army besiege me, my heart will not fear; though war
break out against me, even then will I be confident.*

*One thing I ask of the Lord, this is what I seek: that I may
dwell in the house of the Lord all the days of my life, to gaze upon the beauty of the Lord and to seek him in his temple. For in
the day of trouble he will keep me safe in his dwelling; he will
hide me in the shelter of his tabernacle and set me high upon a
rock. Then my head will be exalted above the enemies who surround me; at his tabernacle will I sacrifice with shouts of joy; I
will sing and make music to the Lord.*

*Hear my voice when I call, O Lord; be merciful to me and
answer me. My heart says of you, "Seek his face!" Your face,
Lord, I will seek. Do not hide your face from me, do not turn
your servant away in anger; you have been my helper. Do not reject me or forsake me, O God my Savior. Though my father and
mother forsake me, the Lord will receive me. Teach me your way,
O Lord; lead me in a straight path because of my oppressors. Do
not turn me over to the desire of my foes, for false witnesses rise
up against me, breathing out violence.*

I am still confident of this: I will see the goodness of the Lord in the land of the living. Wait for the Lord; be strong and take heart and wait for the Lord.

—Psalm 27

He was an awesome sight: over nine feet tall, 200 pounds of armor, and a booming voice that could peal the bark off a tree. David's brothers and their fellow soldiers weren't merely intimidated. They were paralyzed with fear as they watched Goliath strut across the valley. These were fighting men, throwing verbal barbs at one another, daring each other to accept the big man's challenge. Yet deep in their hearts they knew the truth. There wasn't a man in Israel's army worthy to step into the ring with Goliath, let alone go 10 rounds and defeat him.

Ten miles away, David, the youngest of eight boys, the baby of the family, left home to visit his brothers. He was no coward. While tending his father's sheep, he had faced both a bear and a lion and had defeated them soundly. Now David listened as Goliath mocked Israel's army and, worse, Israel's God. Something had to be done. Afraid? Of course. David knew what the giant's sword could do. But he resorted to the weapons that had brought him victory in the past—a slingshot and a faith in the God who is stronger than giants.

You know the rest of the story. All it took was just one stone and a prayer, and the enemy was stretched out—all nine plus feet of him—dead.

Faith has the power to conquer fear.

No one escapes the grip of fear—not the heavyweight boxing champs, not the Einsteins, not the beauty queens. I identify with the little boy who was given a single line in the school play. The speech was simple: "It is I. Be not afraid." But stage fright swept over the small lad in waves. When the teacher pushed him onto the stage, he squeaked, "It's me, and I'm scared!"

How should we handle fear? Let's hear from the man who confronted a giant and lived to tell about it. David tells how God can help us face our fears and win.

A DIVINE BODYGUARD

The Lord is the stronghold of my life—of whom shall I be afraid? (v. 1).

Having a bodyguard has become part of the mystique in the lifestyles of the rich and famous. In many cases, celebrities need protection from people who want to pry into their privacy. Wealthy families are prime targets for kidnapping and extortion. If you are like me, you probably lack the money and the status to have to seriously consider hiring someone to protect your life.

Good news! You already have an around-the-clock service watching out for your good! God himself is our Protector.

From David's background as an army commander, he describes God's work in military terms. **The Lord is my light** (v. 1) reveals the enemy. In the darkness unknown dragons lie in wait. Our fear of the dark often begins in childhood when a vivid imagination can create terrible monsters in the closet or under the bed. Gary Larson, with "The Far Side" cartoons, has a way of putting a different twist to our fears. In one, he drew a bed with a child sleeping on top and two grotesque monsters underneath. One of the monsters says to the other, "I tell you—I heard something moving up above!"

The best antidote for fear of the dark is light. That's why manufacturers market children's night-lights in the shape of clowns and elephants.

God's light reveals our enemy, the devil, for what he really is: a defeated foe. He goes around roaring like a lion. Yet David knew that, with God's help, even lions could be defeated.

The Protector God is **my salvation** (v. 1). His security

41

provides active, offensive deliverance and rescue. The whole world witnessed the awesome firepower of the U.S. military machine during the 1991 Desert Storm conflict. It was offensive action, not negotiation, that finally convinced Saddam Hussein to ask for a truce.

There are times when the only course of action is to do battle with your fears. Perhaps you are fighting an addiction that has made you a captive. Take the offensive. Get help. Recognize that God is standing by to give you courage and to supply the supernatural strength you need to overcome.

God also provides a defensive **stronghold of my life** (v. 1). I love to watch great quarterbacks drop back to throw the long pass to a wide receiver streaking down the sideline. There is no more exciting play in football. However, any NFL quarterback will tell you that his job would be impossible without the blocking of the five offensive linemen. The quarterback may be the hero, but the game is won in the trenches by those who do the blocking and protecting.

When the enemy of fear attacks, threatening to grind you up or stomp you down, God's defensive posture goes into action. Ps. 91:11 promises, **For he will command his angels concerning you to guard you in all your ways.**

With God as your protector, you need not be intimidated by your fears. David was not afraid of the enemy's heaviest artillery. **Even then will I be confident** (v. 3), he declared. You may say, "But my fears are so real, so formidable." That is true. Don't underestimate the enemy. But you can be secure, knowing that God, your Protector, is just as real.

THE NEARNESS OF YOU

One thing I ask . . . that I may dwell in the house of the Lord (v. 4).

Fear is intensified when faced alone. It is diminished when shared with someone. A young boy was asleep until a thunderstorm lit up his attic room with intermittent flashes of light. The thunder sounded as if a howitzer cannon straddled the roof. His mother responded to his cries of fear. As she sat on his bedside, she assured him, "God is right here in your room, and He will take care of you."

"Well, you stay up here with God!" he replied. "I want to go down and sleep with Daddy."

David realized that when we are afraid, our desires become more focused. In verse 4 he makes his request boldly: **One thing I ask of the Lord.** What was that one thing? He didn't ask for money or power. He simply wanted to be where God was: **that I may dwell in the house of the Lord.** David wasn't asking to move into the Tabernacle. He was asking for God to stand with him as he faced his fears.

This was no foxhole prayer. David wasn't requesting God to stand by just until the worst was over. David wanted real fellowship with God. **All the days of my life,** he prayed. He also desired for intimacy in his request: **to gaze upon the beauty of the Lord.** David's heart cry is, "I want to get to know You better, God." That's a good prayer for all of us to pray if we want God to be with us.

Do you want to know God intimately, or is your interest merely in what He can do for you? Ask yourself if you want a rescuer or a relationship.

To God, personal friendship constitutes more than saving you from your fears. He created you to enjoy a rich, meaningful relationship with Him. As He helps you through the hard times, fellowship becomes more meaningful. David wrote in Ps. 16:11, **You will fill me with *joy in your presence*** (emphasis added). What a privilege to know the God of the Universe as a friend!

A LISTENING EAR

Hear my voice when I call, O Lord (v. 7).

When I am afraid, I not only need someone close by but also need a listening ear. Can you sense the urgency in

David's cry for help? He didn't want his prayer to be merely sounds that disappeared in the wind.

One of my favorite stories involves a man walking on a mountain path late at night. He slipped off the edge and began falling down a sharp embankment. In desperation he grabbed a small tree growing out from the cliff. There he hung in the blackness of the night, legs dangling helplessly in midair. He cried out in fear, "Is anybody up there?"

A voice from up above answered, "Yes, I am here. Do you want me to help you?"

The man yelled, "Oh, yes! Please help me!"

"Very well. There is a ledge right below you. Just let go and you'll be safe."

The desperate man paused for a moment, then said, "Is there anybody else up there?"

We need to know that on the other end of the prayer line is a God who never has a busy signal. In fact, at this moment He is sitting by the phone, waiting for us to dial His number.

David may have voiced your deepest fear in prayer when he cried, **Do not reject me or forsake me, O God my Savior** (v. 9). Rejection is hard to bear. We may think, What if God hangs up on me because He knows some of the rotten things I've done in the past? Perhaps God thinks my fears are trivial. I haven't talked to Him much recently. Maybe He talks only to the regular customers.

David put that foolishness to rest in verse 10: **Though my father and mother forsake me, the Lord will receive me.** God will never give up on you. He created you. He sent His Son to die for you. He is not about to forget you now.

One issue needs to be faced squarely: Are we willing to listen and then to obey Him? David realized that our Father knows best. He prays in verse 11, **Teach me your way, O Lord.**

It's not easy to ask for help. I am like many men—I'd

rather do anything than ask for directions when I'm driving. One summer, while on vacation, I was driving late at night through a town near my birthplace. I knew this town well, but in the fog I got turned around. I drove on, looking for a familiar landmark that would give me my bearings. Finally, I swallowed my pride, pulled into a convenience store, and asked for help. To my surprise, I had been going in the wrong direction.

God knows what He's doing. He can see into the future of your life. He can see behind the fears that slow your progress. Ask Him for help. After all, He's only a prayer away.

YOU CAN CONQUER FEAR

Wait for the Lord; be strong and take heart and wait for the Lord (v. 14).

My first response when I see a possible solution to a problem is to charge ahead, to do something. I'm like the proverbial man who jumped on his horse and rode off in all directions at once. You too may find it difficult to **wait for the Lord.** It is only as we walk with the Lord that all of His benefits become ours. We shouldn't run ahead. We shouldn't lag too far behind. With God alongside, you can conquer your fears.

Here are two final challenges: First, **be strong.** What might happen in the future can bring fear to our hearts. Joshua took over the leadership reins of a nation of unruly, complaining people. His job was challenging—to cross the Jordan and conquer the Promised Land. In Moses' farewell speech he challenged Joshua: **Be strong and courageous . . . the Lord himself goes before you . . . Do not be afraid; do not be discouraged** (Deut. 31:7-8).

Have the courage to face your fears squarely, honestly. The strength for victory comes not from your might, but from the Lord.

Second, **take heart,** be encouraged. Overcoming fear is a cooperative effort—God's power and our cooperation.

Remember, the greatest of fears, the grave, has already been conquered by Christ. The empty tomb is a reminder that He can bring victory over the other fears that plague you.

TAKE ACTION

What should you do when fear comes? Here are some suggested responses:

1. Face your fear directly. If possible, identify it by name.

2. Turn to God. Don't try to face the battle alone.

3. Trust God. **Wait for the Lord.** Working with Him insures victory.

Father, I turn my fears over to You, knowing that You and I can handle them together.

6

God's Answer for Dealing with Guilt

Blessed is he whose transgressions are forgiven, whose sins are covered. Blessed is the man whose sin the Lord does not count against him and in whose spirit is no deceit.

When I kept silent, my bones wasted away through my groaning all day long. For day and night your hand was heavy upon me; my strength was sapped as in the heat of summer. Selah.

Then I acknowledged my sin to you and did not cover up my iniquity. I said, "I will confess my transgressions to the Lord"—and you forgave the guilt of my sin. Selah.

Therefore let everyone who is godly pray to you while you may be found; surely when the mighty waters rise, they will not reach him. You are my hiding place; you will protect me from trouble and surround me with songs of deliverance. Selah.

I will instruct you and teach you in the way you should go; I will counsel you and watch over you. Do not be like the horse or the mule, which have no understanding but must be controlled by bit and bridle or they will not come to you. Many are the woes of the wicked, but the Lord's unfailing love surrounds the man who trusts in him.

Rejoice in the Lord and be glad, you righteous; sing, all you who are upright in heart!

—Psalm 32

Arthur Conan Doyle, the creator of the literary character Sherlock Holmes, decided to play a joke on 12 of his friends. To each he sent an anonymous telegram with the simple message "Flee at once. All is discovered." Even Doyle was not prepared for the result. Within 24 hours all 12 had fled the country. The average person carries more guilt than he is willing to admit.

David could certainly write about guilt from firsthand experience. Chapter 11 of 2 Samuel records the story of a successful king with too much time on his hands.

It was springtime, the time of the year when kings lead armies into battle. David didn't feel like going, so his army went without him. The evening sky awakened within him a restlessness, and he wandered out onto the balcony. Then he saw her bathing on the rooftop below. David was transfixed by this woman's incredible beauty. If she was aware of his steady gaze, she made no attempt to cover herself.

David inquired discreetly. Her name was Bathsheba. She was married to one of his officers. But David was the king. He had a right to anything in the kingdom. No one could deny him what he wanted. And at that moment there was nothing he wanted more than that woman. David knew it was wrong, but he sent a messenger to get her. When Bathsheba became pregnant, he tried to cover up the situation by having her husband, Uriah, killed in battle. Marrying her would finally make the whole thing legal and proper.

There was one thing David had not counted on: guilt. It consumed him. David's control over his staff kept them from talking. But God knew, and David knew He knew. Finally God confronted David through His prophet Nathan. The moment of truth had arrived. Dealing with guilt is a painful but necessary process toward finding wholeness. David wrote Psalm 32 to help us come to grips with guilt and discover the grace to overcome it.

CREATING GUILT

Why do we feel guilty anyway? Haven't we reached

the place in this enlightened age in which guilt is a thing of the past? Erich Fromm makes the point: "It is indeed amazing that in as fundamentally an irreligious culture as ours, the sense of guilt should be so widespread and deep-rooted as it is." The reason we have not been able to make guilt disappear is that it is real. We have wronged God.

David uses some terms in the first two verses that define what he is talking about. He uses **transgressions** to mean rebellion against God, doing what we shouldn't be doing. The word **sin** is easier to understand. When I sin I fall short of God's standard, either by doing what I shouldn't or failing to do what I should. David also utilizes the term **deceit** to describe the big cover-up when guilt occurs. Given a little time, we assume that guilt should go away. Instead, it stays.

Why does God make you feel guilty? Is He out to steal all the joy of life? Does He gain some kind of satisfaction from seeing you squirm? No! God does not have a masochistic streak. He wants to bring about a change in your life. Guilt is designed to get you to stop doing wrong.

Is it fair for God to make me feel miserable just so that I will change my behavior? Imagine yourself in the kitchen next to the red glow of a stove burner. You accidentally let your hand rest on that hot burner. Immediately the nerves in your hand send a strong message that sets off bells and whistles in the brain. The pain makes you pull your hand away quickly. Is the pain good for you? You might be tempted to say no as your hand throbs. But without the pain your hand would have suffered far greater damage. Guilt, even though painful, is of great benefit if it can get you to move away from destructive activity.

CONCEALING GUILT

David responded the same way most of us do when we feel guilty—he hid his wrongdoing. By his own admission he said, **I kept silent** (v. 3). But burying guilt does not get rid of it. Unresolved guilt is like toxic waste hidden just below the topsoil. Sooner or later the problem will rise to the surface.

Concealing guilt can have physical consequences. David admitted that his **bones wasted away** (v. 3). Famous psychiatrist Karl Menninger of the Menninger Clinic said that 75 percent of the psychiatric hospital patients could walk out of the hospital the next day if they knew their sins were forgiven.

Guilt takes a tremendous emotional toll. David described the inner pain **as my groaning all day long** (v. 3). In verse 4 he said, **My strength was sapped.** It takes large amounts of emotional energy just to deal with guilt on a day-after-day basis. The time and effort wasted by guilt-induced worrying could better be used for something constructive.

However, we can't overlook the spiritual dimension. David was aware that God knew his secret. **For day and night your hand was heavy upon me** (v. 4). God simply will not let us sweep our guilt under the rug and forget it. Part of the work of the Holy Spirit is to **convict the world of guilt in regard to sin** (John 16:8).

Although we may wish it weren't so, concealed sin is bound to surface. Edgar Allan Poe used this truth in his story of "The Tell-Tale Heart." The murderer buried the body of his victim under the floorboards of his house. No one would ever know. But the guilty man could hear the beating of the dead man's heart right through the wooden floor. Thump! Thump! Thump! Thump! Finally he couldn't take it anymore. You can't cover up guilt forever.

CONFESSING GUILT

What do you do with a guilty conscience? Wouldn't it be nice to be able to go back and change some of those painful memories? But let's be realistic. We have no power to go back and undo the sins of the past. We must confront guilt in the present. David gives help in the way he faced the problem. Three phrases in verse 5 offer guidance to us:

Then I acknowledged my sin to you. The first step to freedom is seeing sin as God sees it. If I continue to rationalize my actions, I fool no one but myself. Last summer a large brown spot began to grow in my nice green yard. I ignored the spot at first, but it kept on enlarging. I poured extra water there, thinking the roots needed more moisture. In the back of my mind I knew the real problem. Billbugs had gotten down in my lawn, feasting on the precious roots of the grass. When I finally faced the reality of the problem, I was ready to do something about it. One call to my lawn specialist, and the problem was attacked—right at the root.

I . . . did not cover up my iniquity. This is no time for rationalizing. The devil did not make me do it. He may have tempted me, but *I* made the rational choice to disobey. When confronting sin, don't say, "I did it, but . . ." God knows the truth, and it's time we own up to it.

I will confess my transgressions to the Lord. This is not the confession of the boy who is caught with his hand in the cookie jar. He may say he is sorry. However, his only real sorrow is that he has been caught. David is communicating a profound sorrow for what he has done. Just feeling bad is not enough. The Bible uses the term repentance. Repentance means that we turn away from our sin and follow God. Zacchaeus, the little tax collector who met Jesus in a tree, grasped the need for repentance. He told Jesus, **Look, Lord! Here and now I give half of my possessions to the poor, and if I have cheated anybody out of anything, I will pay back four times the amount** (Luke 19:8). Repentance is real when it results in action.

CANCELING GUILT

The Bible has good news for us when it comes to our guilt. As hard as it is to believe, God forgives us for our wrongdoing. For David, this was personal. As verse 5 concludes, you can sense David's gratitude: **You forgave the guilt of my sin.** The guilt that had weighed heavily upon his shoulders was suddenly lifted.

51

In David's day, obtaining forgiveness for sin was a complicated matter. Once a year, a goat was selected by the high priest. The priest placed his hands on the head of the goat and confessed all the sins of the people. That innocent animal symbolically received the guilt of the nation. To illustrate that the guilt was gone, he was sent into the wilderness. The goat was a scapegoat to bear the corporate wrongdoing of all the people.

For us, Christ became a scapegoat. The combined guilt of all our sins was placed on Him as He died for us on the Cross. Sin is not a casual issue to God. Our guilt caused His Son to suffer a horrible death. Only because Jesus loved us was He willing to pay such a price for our freedom from guilt.

God not only has forgiven our guilt but has forgotten our sins. We all have things in our past that, if revealed publicly, would make us want to crawl into a hole and die. How could God know such horrible facts about us and still want us as children? The Bible tells us that God chooses not to remember. God's words through the prophet Jeremiah allow us to breathe a sigh of relief: **For I will forgive their wickedness and will remember their sins no more** (31:34). There is an unmarked grave in Sidney, N.Y., that has but one word—"Forgiven." That says it all.

If the guilt is truly gone, you have reason to celebrate. David ends his psalm with **Rejoice in the Lord and be glad, you righteous** (v. 11). You are **righteous** if you have been forgiven. The guilt is gone. It's time to run, shout, and celebrate. You have been set free!

———

TAKE ACTION

1. Reread David's prayer for forgiveness, Psalm 51, to see how desperately he wanted to have his guilt removed and his relationship with God restored. If you have unconfessed sin, ask Jesus to cleanse away that sin with His blood.

2. Once you have asked God to forgive you, accept His cleansing. Asking God time and time again for forgiveness for the same sin is showing a lack of faith. When God forgives, He forgets. Perhaps you need to forgive yourself.

3. Share the good news that God forgives sins with someone who needs forgiveness.

Thank You, Father, for taking away my guilt when You forgave my sins.

7

God's Answer for Your Worry

Do not fret because of evil men or be envious of those who do wrong; for like the grass they will soon wither, like green plants they will soon die away.

Trust in the Lord and do good; dwell in the land and enjoy safe pasture. Delight yourself in the Lord and he will give you the desires of your heart.

Commit your way to the Lord; trust in him and he will do this: He will make your righteousness shine like the dawn, the justice of your cause like the noonday sun.

Be still before the Lord and wait patiently for him; do not fret when men succeed in their ways, when they carry out their wicked schemes.

—Psalm 37:1-7

Do you ever worry? If you answered "No," you can skip this chapter and go read a book on lying to yourself. Seriously, worry is a problem that affects anyone who is aware of what is going on in life. American poet Robert Frost was quoted as saying, "The reason why worry kills more people than work does is that more people worry than work."

Some worry is a normal part of life. If my teenage

daughter were driving the car alone on a snowy evening and was two hours late, I would worry. She might have had car trouble or been in an accident. A burning log rolling out of my fireplace and onto the rug would worry me. Unconcern could cost me my house. Worry is part of the cost of being alive and loving other people.

But it is possible to worry to the extent that you cannot function properly. Psalm 37 speaks words of help and encouragement to those who are crippled by worry. The writer, David, begins with the words **Do not fret**. The phrase could be literally translated, "Don't get heated or burned up with anger." We all know those feelings of heartburn that come when we become anxious with worry. It is easy to talk about not worrying. The issue is—how can we stop?

In this psalm we are reminded that God is interested in the things that worry us. His care at our "worry points" can bring us victory over worry.

LIFE IS SO DAILY

Does God really care about the mundane events of our lives? I once heard someone observe: "The problem with life is that it is so daily." We can be sure that the monthly bills will arrive on time. In the unlikely event that the post office loses a bill, be assured that another one will arrive next month with a service charge added.

Is it possible to keep from worrying about the food bills and the clothing costs? Apparently Jesus thought so. In His Sermon on the Mount in Matthew 6, He talks about God feeding the birds of the air and clothing the grass of the field. His directive: **But seek first his kingdom and his righteousness, and all these things will be given to you as well. Therefore do not worry** (vv. 33-34).

David's word in verse 3 is **Trust in the Lord.** We can believe that God will do His part. Trust is the confidence that God can and will act. A little boy wrote the following letter to God: "Dear God, If You do all these things, You are pretty busy. Now, here's my question. When is the best time to talk to You? When will You be listening hard in Troy, New York? Sincerely, Allen." God is not only listening hard in Troy but is awaiting our prayers wherever we are.

We have a part to play in living victoriously as well. David continues by saying, **Do good.** Taking action on the things we can will help worry subside. I have discovered that some of my worries come as a result of poor planning or of procrastination. For instance, after the lights are out, my wife will say, "Are the doors locked?" I will try to remember if I checked the doors. Then I will estimate that there is a 75% chance that they are locked. But, what if the door is open and someone comes in? I can either lie there and worry about the doors, or I can get up and make sure they are locked. Praying about the doors is not enough. I need to check them all personally.

If we trust God to do His part, and then do all we can do, we can relax and enjoy life. Verse 3 ends with **enjoy safe pasture.** God has provided for our needs and our safety. Why not quit worrying so much and enjoy? The old hymn is still true: "Trust and obey, For there's no other way / To be happy in Jesus But to trust and obey" (John H. Sammis).

WHAT ABOUT YOUR HEART?

God also cares about our choices. I'm not sure God has a strong opinion on whether I order a hamburger or pizza for lunch. But desires of the heart are a different matter. Verse 4 gets to the point: **Delight yourself in the Lord and he will give you the desires of your heart.**

What we delight in determines what we worry about. To put it another way, our delights become our goals— what we really care about. If you are a young person and delight in staying physically young, you will worry about gray hair or wrinkles. If your goal is gaining wealth, you will worry about how to get rich, and how to protect your money once you have it in your possession.

One man I know set as his life goal the making of money. While he used many legitimate means to provide for financial security, the money wasn't coming fast enough. He decided to cut some legal corners. His conscience was in conflict because his unethical business dealings clashed with his moral upbringing. Finally, the man was caught and arrested—he really had reason to worry then. His problem was clear. The desires of his heart had become unbalanced.

When we delight in the Lord, worry is replaced by joy. God is the Source of every good gift. When we have Him, we have all we need.

Delighting in the Lord brings with it new desires. When I was 14 years old, a friend of mine in the church came home from his freshman year of college to earn some money. He bought a dilapidated 1932 Ford five-window coupe to restore in his extra time. I loved hot rods, and this was the perfect car for that purpose. Soon we were spending every night disassembling the car piece by piece. This was going to be the most beautiful street rod in the area. Just as we were about to put the car back together, my mechanic partner met a girl. Instead of spending time working on the car, he started spending all his time with her. Soon they were engaged, and the wonderful car project was put up for sale. My friend's delight was now in being with his girl. All he wanted to do was to make her happy.

When we find our happiness in Jesus, we want the things that will please Him. If your heart is at one with God's, it is no risk for God to give you whatever your heart desires.

WHAT WILL PEOPLE THINK?

Many people are crippled by worry about what others think of them. It may be a natural reaction to be concerned about what people think, especially when our moral character is unfairly attacked. We may feel the injustice of the situation. We think: How could my accusers know the inner motives of my heart? How could those lies about me be believed? What if folks never learn the real truth about me? Sometimes life isn't fair.

You're not alone with those thoughts. Jesus was also falsely accused. His enemies called Him everything from a glutton and drunkard to a blasphemer. How did Jesus respond when people slandered His character? First Pet. 2:23 reads, **When they hurled their insults at him, he did not retaliate; when he suffered, he made no threats. Instead, he entrusted himself to him who judges justly.**

David tells us: **Commit your way [literally, "roll your way of life"] to the Lord: trust in him and he will do this: He will make your righteousness shine like the dawn, the justice of your cause like the noonday sun** (vv. 5-6). Put yourself in the Father's hands just as Jesus **entrusted himself.**

God has a way of vindicating unjust attacks. He knows our hearts even if no one else knows or understands. Consider Joseph's case. First he had these wonderful dreams about sheaves of grain and the sun, moon, and 11 stars bowing down before him. Imagine Joseph's frustration when he was next sold as a slave to some Egyptian traders. Then, just about the time things began looking up for him, he was falsely accused of assaulting his master's wife. Joseph found himself sitting in a dark prison cell, innocent yet forgotten. But *God* had not forgotten him. Injustice became the inroad to Joseph's vindication and his eventual elevation to the prime minister's office of Egypt. Joseph did not harbor a hint of bitterness toward his brothers, his boss, or even God. The Father is fully capable of working out injustices. Worry, on the other hand, has no power to right wrongs.

BAD THINGS CAN HAPPEN
TO GOOD PEOPLE

God cares about our concerns. There are problems that hit like a sledgehammer between the eyes. The very words *cancer, stroke, heart attack,* or *surgery* can create a burning in the pits of our stomachs. Relational family crises such as a runaway teen, threats of divorce, or the financial collapse of a retirement program can be devastating. It doesn't take much for worry to begin to overwhelm us in those kinds of situations.

When such shocking developments strike, a certain amount of concern is normal. It doesn't mean that we have lost our spiritual moorings if anxiety sweeps over us like a tidal wave. The issue is how we respond to the crisis and the feelings that accompany it.

Verse 7 can be more effective than any tranquilizing pill when worry strikes. **Be still before the Lord and wait patiently for him.** While it may be necessary to take quick action, my inner being can be waiting before God.

This was made forcefully clear to me on a day that changed the direction of my whole life. I was about to begin my last year of seminary. My wife, Jackie, had a good job teaching school. I was having a wonderful time working as an assistant pastor in a growing church. Suddenly, my tranquil world was shattered. Jackie was seriously injured in a car accident and was barely clinging to life. My surroundings seemed distant and unreal as my senior pastor drove me 20 miles to the Kansas City hospital. I was confronted with the very real possibility that I could lose my dear wife and companion of four years. Worry swept over me with such force that I thought I would die myself.

The second hand moved in slow motion as I sat in the waiting room. The doctors were doing all that was humanly possible to keep her alive. I sat there numb, talking quietly to God. "Father," I silently prayed, "You know that she's Yours." Then God spoke in a voice that was inaudible, but as clear and unmistakable as I have ever heard. He said to me, "If she's Mine, then let Me have her."

The implication was clear. To say yes to God's will meant I couldn't demand my will. I took a deep breath and said, "OK, God." At that moment a sense of peace swept over me. I still didn't know how it would all turn out. There was no real assurance that she would even make it through the crisis. But I knew that God was in charge, and He would do what was best. Worry began to dissolve as I waited on the Lord.

After 10 days of unconsciousness, Jackie woke up. She spent six weeks in the hospital and has undergone three hip surgeries in the years since. However, the Lord has been with her, giving her a life of fulfilling ministry. What worry could never have accomplished, God brought about because we put our trust in Him.

Someone who understood the toll of worry made this quip: "To take care to bed is to sleep with a pack on your back." The same can be said for carrying worry through the day. Imprint the words **Do not fret** on the inside of your forehead during the day and on the inside of your eyelids at night. God is with you. That's all you need to know.

TAKE ACTION

1. List on a piece of paper the things that currently cause you to worry. Turn your paper upside down. Imagine that God has taken the worries from you.

2. Memorize Phil. 4:6-7. Quote it whenever you begin to worry.

Father, thank You for being at my "worry points" with Your presence. Amen.

8

God's Answer for Your Feelings of Depression

As the deer pants for streams of water, so my soul pants for you, O God. My soul thirsts for God, for the living God. When can I go and meet with God? My tears have been my food day and night, while men say to me all day long, "Where is your God?" These things I remember as I pour out my soul: how I used to go with the multitude, leading the procession to the house of God, with shouts of joy and thanksgiving among the festive throng.

Why are you downcast, O my soul? Why so disturbed within me? Put your hope in God, for I will yet praise him, my Savior and my God.

My soul is downcast within me; therefore I will remember you from the land of the Jordan, the heights of Hermon—from Mount Mizar. Deep calls to deep in the roar of your waterfalls; all your waves and breakers have swept over me.

By day the Lord directs his love, at night his song is with me—a prayer to the God of my life.

I say to God my Rock, "Why have you forgotten me? Why must I go about mourning, oppressed by the enemy?" My bones suffer mortal agony as my foes taunt me, saying to me all day long, "Where is your God?"

Why are you downcast, O my soul? Why so disturbed with-

in me? Put your hope in God, for I will yet praise him, my Savior and my God.

—Psalm 42

Vindicate me, O God, and plead my cause against an ungodly nation; rescue me from deceitful and wicked men. You are God my stronghold. Why have you rejected me? Why must I go about mourning, oppressed by the enemy? Send forth your light and your truth, let them guide me; let them bring me to your holy mountain, to the place where you dwell. Then will I go to the altar of God, to God, my joy and my delight. I will praise you with the harp, O God, my God.

Why are you downcast, O my soul? Why so disturbed within me? Put your hope in God, for I will yet praise him, my Savior and my God.

—Psalm 43

Sun Valley, Idaho, is one of the most inviting settings in America. Nestled in a mountain valley, it is well known for winter skiing and summer fishing. From the beginning of its commercial development, Sun Valley has been the playground for the rich and famous. This perfect setting compelled Ernest Hemingway to build a home there in an attempt to find inner peace. The author was known both for his writing genius and his adventuresome lifestyle. Yet with all he had going for him, he suffered from bouts of severe depression. The beautiful scenery of Sun Valley was no antidote for the despair of his soul. On July 2, 1961, he took his favorite shotgun and put an end to his despair by taking his own life.

Depression can also affect the lives of spiritual giants. The great English preacher Charles Spurgeon was well known for his wonderful sense of humor. However, Spurgeon also suffered deep, anguishing depression caused by a physical problem.

What is depression? Psychologists define it as a sense of sadness, dejection, despair, or hopelessness, often caused by the loss of something valuable. When you get depressed, you lose interest in your surroundings. It becomes difficult to cope with even routine activities. You feel like drawing the covers up to your ears—anything to avoid people and life in general.

Depression is a common problem. Probably sometime in your life you will experience depression. One out of eight Americans will find that the problem is so severe it requires professional treatment.

Christians have not always had a clear understanding of depression. Some have thought that it is a sin to be handled by confession and faith. Others have held that these feelings are simply in the mind—if you cheer up and think positive thoughts, the problem will vanish. Anyone who has felt the grip of depression knows that the answers are not that easy.

The author of Psalms 42 and 43 experienced depression firsthand. Let's look at some of the signals he gives.

MIND GAMES

The Psalmist reviews his sadness over something very precious that has been taken away—his freedom to worship. In 42:4 he muses, **How I used to go with the multitude, leading the procession to the house of God, with shouts of joy and thanksgiving among the festive throng.** Mental stress can lead to fatigue and depression. What used to be important to us is now insignificant.

Although Moses was an excellent leader, he became discouraged and depressed as he tried to guide his people through the desert. The whining and complaining over the lack of meat was more than he could stand. He cried out to God in Num. 11:13-15, **They keep wailing to me, "Give us meat to eat!" I cannot carry all these people by myself; the burden is too heavy for me. If this is how you are going to treat me, put me to death right now.** When you are depressed, even death looks inviting. Moses' task was more than he could handle alone. God's answer to him was simple: he was to recruit 70 men to help him. Imagine! Moses had been trying to do the work of 70! God does not expect that kind of effort from Moses—or you.

FEELING THE BLUES

The Psalmist also relates an emotional signal of depression: **My tears have been my food day and night** (42:3). God created us as emotional creatures. Emotions are much like ocean waves. For every high there will be a corresponding low following later. Certain personality types are especially prone to emotional highs and lows.

Elijah was one who experienced both the thrill of victory and the agony of defeat. Imagine the emotional high of seeing the defeat of 850 false prophets on Mount Carmel! He was so pumped up that he raced 20 miles down the mountain ahead of King Ahab.

But when Queen Jezebel heard that her 850 prophets were dead and she put out a contract for Elijah's life, his emotions fell like a rock! Out in the desert, alone and depressed, Elijah wanted to die. The enemy was too powerful. God had forgotten him. Elijah, I think, must have been the inventor of the martyr complex.

God understood Elijah's problem. He gave no lectures or pep talks. Instead, He put Elijah to sleep. With his emotions rested, he was a new man.

Our emotions can tire as easily as our bodies. That is the reason God planned a Sabbath day of rest when He created the world. We all need to recharge our physical and emotional batteries once every seven days. Everyone needs a periodic vacation. Recreation allows you to re-create your emotional storehouse.

MY BODY CAN'T KEEP UP

The physical body sends clear signals when we are depressed. The writer of this psalm lost his appetite. **My** tears have been my food day and night (42:3). His body ached deep within: **My bones suffer mortal agony** (42:10). When depression hits, your body is the first to know.

It is possible for the chemistry within your body to change and cause you to experience depression. Perhaps your brain or one of your glands malfunctions. Suddenly you feel unexplained depression. Up to 80 percent of new mothers suffer from postpartum depression after giving birth. Many who suffer from certain illnesses also have depression as an accompanying symptom.

You are probably familiar with the problems of Job. He lost all his children, livestock, and servants in a single day. Later he battled the excruciating pain of sores from head to toe. The physical and mental losses sent him into an emotional tailspin. Job suffered the classic signs of depression: **For sighing comes to me instead of food; my groans pour out like water** (3:24). However, you have to admire Job's spiritual tenacity. In the midst of his suffering, he continued to claim God's goodness.

WHERE IS GOD?

When depression strikes, God usually seems far away. The Psalmist asks God, **Why have you rejected me?** (43:2). At the moment when you need the reassuring intimacy of God's presence, He is nowhere to be found. Depression can leave you feeling spiritually bankrupt.

Jonah is notorious for his famous fish ride. But what about the rest of the story? He was angry at God for sending him to Nineveh. With God's thumb pressing on his backbone, Jonah preached his heart out. The results were beyond belief. The city repented and returned to God. Jonah stewed in bitterness as Nineveh rejoiced in revival. The prophet wanted the wicked city punished, not saved. He turned his face toward God and shouted, **I am angry enough to die!** (4:9). The book ends without any resolution to Jonah's problem. Spiritual depression will remain unsolved unless you resolve your differences with God.

WHEN DEPRESSION STRIKES

No one ever experiences just a slight depression. When you are depressed, it's a serious matter. There are some steps you can take to overcome this problem.

Deal with the physical. Help your body by getting enough rest. Eat nourishing food. If symptoms continue, have a physical checkup by a physician. Once I had an employee who suffered with several symptoms of depression. I suggested she discuss her problem with her doctor. Tests showed a physical disorder that could be corrected by treatment and medication. In no time she was feeling normal again.

Learn to recognize the role your emotions may have in depression. Ps. 42:7 says, **Deep calls to deep.** When you hurt in the deepest part of your being, you need to get it out. Sometimes it helps to share those deep feelings with another person. You may find understanding from a close friend.

One person put the following ad in a local paper: "For $5.00 I will listen to you talk for 30 minutes without making comment." The results were beyond expectation. The man was soon receiving 10 to 20 calls a day.

Don't reject the possibility of professional counseling. God uses healing professionals to bring wholeness to damaged emotions. Remember, God cares and understands. He will listen to your deepest heart cries. Think again of the words of that familiar hymn: "O Love that will not let me go, / I rest my weary soul in Thee" (George Matheson).

Take a new look at your mental outlook. Depression can develop when you harbor negative mental attitudes. The Psalmist talked to himself: **Why are you downcast, O my soul? Why so disturbed within me?** (42:5). Begin right now to develop a positive mental attitude. It's not difficult. If you have a tendency to look on the dark side, memorize Phil. 4:8—**Whatever is true, whatever is noble, whatever is right, whatever is pure, whatever is lovely, whatever is admirable—if anything is excellent or praiseworthy—think about such things.**

If you are battling depression, don't neglect the spiritual dimension of your life. Psalm 42 contains several faith builders:

I will remember you (v. 6). God has not abandoned you.

Put your hope in God (v. 5). God has the power to deliver you.

I will yet praise Him (v. 5). Praise changes the focus from your problem to God's solution.

You may be in the pit of depression. Your first step back to normalcy is to recognize that God cares and understands.

A middle-aged man once came into my office in the grips of deep depression. In the past he had served the Lord. But through a combination of events he had abandoned his faith. Now he was at the end of his emotional tether. I shared with him how he could know God's forgiveness and receive His help. He made the first faltering step of faith back to God that day. Very slowly he began to trust God with his failures and fears. Within a few weeks, his depression vanished. In its place was a new joy. Hope replaced despair. He now had a purpose for living. Jesus made the difference.

Even if you feel the situation is hopeless, there is hope for you. Seek deliverance from whatever source God provides you. Jesus cares. The moment you ask, help is on the way.

TAKE ACTION

1. If you are battling depression, check out the physical, mental, and spiritual aspects of your life. Don't hesitate to consult professionals if necessary.

2. Be a supportive listener and encourager to a friend who is depressed.

Father, thank You for understanding my moods and being there to help. Amen.

9

God's Answer for Your Stress

God is our refuge and strength, an ever-present help in trouble. Therefore we will not fear, though the earth give way and the mountains fall into the heart of the sea, though its waters roar and foam and the mountains quake with their surging. Selah.

There is a river whose streams make glad the city of God, the holy place where the Most High dwells. God is within her, she will not fall; God will help her at break of day. Nations are in uproar, kingdoms fall; he lifts his voice, the earth melts.

The Lord Almighty is with us; the God of Jacob is our fortress. Selah.

Come and see the works of the Lord, the desolations he has brought on the earth. He makes wars cease to the ends of the earth; he breaks the bow and shatters the spear, he burns the shields with fire. "Be still, and know that I am God; I will be exalted among the nations, I will be exalted in the earth."

The Lord Almighty is with us; the God of Jacob is our fortress. Selah.

—Psalm 46

I needed to catch a plane home from Denver. That's usually not much of a problem in the Mile-High City unless it snows.

I awoke that morning to find four inches covering the ground. It's amazing how easily fluffy flakes in the air can slow two-ton cars to a snail's pace. My sister, who was driving me to the airport, suggested that we ought to allow a few extra minutes for traffic. What an understatement! The normal 30-minute drive turned into an hour and 40 minutes of demolition derby.

A voice inside me yelled, "Drive on the shoulder! Cut across the field! Run a stoplight! Don't you people know I have a plane to catch?"

All I could do was sit on the right front seat with my white knuckles squeezing the life out of the dashboard. About 15 minutes from the airport I glanced at my watch, thinking that at that moment the stewardess was probably closing the door of the plane. Seat 11-C would be vacant. Mentally, I began to rearrange my busy schedule. When would the next flight leave for Boise?

As the car pulled up to the terminal, I leaped out, grabbed my luggage, and dashed for the ticket counter. The departures lit up the video screen suspended from the ceiling. I checked the status of my flight to Boise—the plane hadn't even arrived yet from Omaha! I wouldn't leave for another hour. All my stress had been wasted energy.

The synonyms for stress are very familiar: *strain, pressure, tension*. The word comes from the Latin *strictus*, meaning "to be drawn tight." Mention stress and the mind produces vivid images: racing heartbeat, rising blood pressure, sweaty palms, burning stomach, razor-edged nerves. In the heat of stress, emotions are stretched like a rubber band, ready to snap. I'm uneasy just thinking about it.

Everyone experiences stress in one form or another. And not all stress is bad. We need a certain amount of it to stimulate creativity and growth. A history test can be stressful to a student. However, a failing grade on a report card could be even more stressful. The stress brought on by an upcoming test can motivate an otherwise lazy boy to study history.

The tone of a violin is dependent on stress. That top string is stretched until it will vibrate to the pitch of E. With not enough stress it sounds muddy. Pull the string too tightly, and it snaps.

STRESSED OUT

What are the causes of stress? Any change from the normal patterns of life can be stressful. That sweet, cuddly baby demands 2 A.M. feedings and periodic diaper changing. Retirement can mean real stress for the wife who is not used to having her husband underfoot every day.

Conflicts breed stress. Nowhere is conflict more intense than on the job. Stress from a demanding boss or unrealistic job expectations can make you physically ill. Neither are the home or the church safe havens from conflict. A church board member once told me, "I couldn't sleep at all last night because I was thinking about the discussion during the board meeting."

Overcommitments can generate the feeling that life is out of control. The mother who serves as taxi driver, dietitian, recreation director, housekeeper, nurse, teacher, and confidante for the family is bound to feel overwhelmed at times. The same goes for the father who pushes himself to climb the corporate ladder while coaching Little League and working for the United Way. Sometime we identify with the juggler who is trying to keep all the plates spinning on his sticks.

Stress has a way of overwhelming us—pressures, schedules, expectations. The demands of life grab and pull at our insides until we feel we are up to our necks in a pit of snapping alligators.

Have you ever wondered why a lion tamer takes a wooden chair into a cage? It's certainly not for protection. One swipe of a lion's paw and the chair would become a pile of toothpicks. The trainer pushes the four legs toward the lion's face. To the lion the wooden legs represent four foes. Though he is the King of the Beasts, he can't focus on all four at once. As a result, the lion becomes confused and disabled, easily controlled by the trainer.

Satan uses the confusion brought about by stress to render us ineffective and make us more susceptible to his suggestions.

Psalm 46 is a song for stressed people. This is not self-help music. After all, you and I are the ones who got ourselves into the mess of stress. Only God can help. And that is the whole point of the song. Here are three promises from a God who is concerned about the tensions in your life.

GOD'S PROTECTION

God is our refuge and strength, an ever-present help in trouble (v. 1).

We live in a world suffering from the aftershocks of man's fall. We can't read a newspaper without being reminded of the almost daily disasters that leave humans suffering. It is terrifying to see the forces of nature unleashed.

God clearly acknowledges our tendency to fear: **Therefore we will not fear, though the earth give way** (v. 2).

I like to think that the earth is solid, dependable. But if it moves, where can we stand? The San Francisco earthquake of 1989 was extremely unsettling to Bay Area residents. Families lost homes and loved ones. Lives were changed forever. And school counselors were swamped with children trying to cope with the stress the tragedy brought to their young lives.

And also consider man's cruelty to man. Murder, rape, robbery, and drugs have forced many people to cower behind locked doors or purchase guard dogs.

Nowhere does God promise to take us out of the real world with its threats—at least not while we're alive. He does promise to provide for us a place of defense, **a refuge** (v. 1).

71

Near our home in Idaho is a stretch of land along the Snake River that provides refuge for a large variety of hawks, eagles, falcons, and other birds of prey. Their nests are built securely in cliffs that overlook the river. Storms may come, but the birds are safe in the rocks. Hymn writer William O. Cushing used this imagery when he wrote:

> *Oh, safe to the Rock that is higher than I,*
> *My soul in its conflicts and sorrows would fly. . . .*
> *How often, when trials like sea billows roll,*
> *Have I hidden in Thee, O Thou Rock of my soul.*

God's protection also provides power to fight. Your source of stress may be none other than Satan himself. He understands the debilitating effect of too much tension. As you face the devil's assault, God is **an ever-present help.** He comes to bring you **strength.**

In God's protection, you can relax and quit worrying. That's the conclusion the Psalmist drew: **Therefore we will not fear** (v. 2).

A man with a morbid fear of thunder visited a psychiatrist to discuss his problem.

"Don't be afraid," the doctor counseled. "Just think of it as a drumroll in the symphony of life."

"What if that doesn't work?"

The psychiatrist answered, "Then do what I do. Stuff your ears with cotton, crawl under the covers, and sing 'Mary Had a Little Lamb' as loud as you can."

Isn't it silly—the things we trust in when we're afraid? God offers us real, genuine protection when we're smack-dab in the middle of life's stresses. File away the words *refuge, strength,* and *ever-present help* for quick reference when you face times of trouble.

GOD'S PRESENCE

The Lord Almighty is with us; the God of Jacob is our fortress (vv. 7, 11).

I vividly remember as a child riding in a northern

Minnesota snowstorm with my dad. The car's headlights illuminated the snowflakes as they rushed past the windshield and into the dark. It was cold outside, but the heater in the car warmed my small body. Most important, my father was there. His presence made everything OK. I put my head on his lap and went to sleep, secure in the middle of a snowstorm.

God's presence comes to us as a sustaining force. The songwriter poetically describes God as **a river** (v. 4). As he writes the music, he remembers the time when Jerusalem was under siege by the enemy. The river was the lifeblood of the city. Without the water from the river, there was no survival.

I imagine the river not as a tiny, bubbling brook but as a broad, powerful, slowly moving force of water. God's presence is a stabilizing force, something you can depend upon.

Growing up next to the Mississippi, I was intrigued by the constant flow of water that was seemingly inexhaustible. The river could be depended upon, no matter what else happened. Jerome Kern captured that idea in the song from the musical *Showboat:* "That Ol' Man River, he just keeps rollin' along."

God is within her (the city of God, or, God's child), **she will not fall** (v. 5). Envision a young toddler trying to make the transition from hands and knees mobility. The little girl stands tottering and shaking, unsure of the next move. Mom or Dad stands in front of her with hands outstretched. All she needs to do is step out and reach for the stabilizing hand. It is strong enough to hold her up.

Winds of stress threaten to blow you over. Those gusts are especially difficult when they come unexpectedly. The blast can take your breath away. But standing with you in the storm is the invisible, yet unmistakable, presence of God. He is there for one reason—to keep you standing. Jude's benediction is my favorite: **To him who is able to keep you from falling and to present you before his glorious presence without fault and with great joy** (v. 24).

Remember, if Jesus is sailing in your boat, the boat won't sink, and the storm won't last forever.

GOD'S PEACE

Be still, and know that I am God (v. 10).

The cottage I am writing in is nestled high in the mountains and overlooks a lovely blue lake. Tall pines almost touch the white, fluffy clouds floating overhead. Chipmunks chatter above the rustle of the aspen leaves. In this setting, peace comes easily. But soon a security man, looking for suspects to a possible cabin break-in, knocks on my door and disturbs the silence. Even the serenity of backwoods country cannot guarantee peace.

The world I live in is very different. Yours is probably different too. Television brings into our homes news of hostage taking, revolutions, tornado casualties, and gang violence in deadly color.

Does God really care about the conflicts that touch your life? Is He on vacation, leaving you to fend for yourself the best you can?

God does act directly in the affairs of men. **He makes wars cease to the ends of the earth; he breaks the bow and shatters the spear, he burns the shields with fire** (v. 9).

But what about the times when He does not directly intervene? Nerves can become frazzled while you wait for Him to ride in and straighten out the mess. God's word to you is **Be still.** But what does **still** mean? The literal meaning of the Hebrew word **still** is "relax."

Jesus looked out across the foaming, frothy waves of Galilee. The wind whipped the lowered sails of the boat until they imitated the sounds of a woodpecker. Experienced seamen gripped the oars until their knuckles were as white as their bulging eyes. Adrenaline surged through their bodies. When the storm had played its loudest crescendo, Jesus faced the wind and simply said, **Quiet! Be**

still! (Mark 4:39). The wind died down, the waves calmed, and in a moment peace was restored.

Stress can whip your emotions to a fever pitch. You may get to the place where you can't take one more thing. Jesus looks out across the churning confusion of your existence and says to your heart, **Quiet! Be still!** His is the Voice of authority. **Be still, and know that I am God**. This is the Creator God speaking. If He promises peace, He can deliver.

God brings peace to the confusion caused by mental and emotional overload. He wants us to deal with stress one issue at a time. He intends for us to live one day at a time. Jesus said, **Therefore do not worry about tomorrow, for tomorrow will worry about itself. Each day has enough trouble of its own** (Matt. 6:34). In other words, we should do our best and leave the rest to Him.

A TIME FOR CHANGE

Too often stress is the result of the unrealistic expectations we place on ourselves. Speaker and writer Tim Hansel speaks of the hard lessons he learned in his journey to live a more stress-free life. In his book *When I Relax I Feel Guilty,* he includes an account of an anonymous friar from a monastery in Nebraska:

> *If I had my life to live over again, I'd try to make more mistakes next time.*
>
> *I would relax, I would limber up, I would be sillier than I have been this trip.*
>
> *I know of very few things I would take seriously.*
>
> *I would take more trips. I would be crazier.*
>
> *I would climb more mountains, swim more rivers, and watch more sunsets.*
>
> *I would do more walking and looking.*
>
> *I would eat more ice cream and less beans.*
>
> *I would have more actual troubles, and fewer imaginary ones.*

You see, I'm one of those people who lives life prophylactically and sensibly hour after hour, day after day. Oh, I've had my moments, and if I had to do it over again I'd have more of them.

In fact, I'd try to have nothing else, just moments, one after another, instead of living so many years ahead each day. I've been one of those people who never go anywhere without a thermometer, a hot-water bottle, a gargle, a raincoat, aspirin, and a parachute.

If I had to do it over again I would go places, do things, and travel lighter than I have.

If I had my life to live over I would start barefooted earlier in the spring and stay that way later in the fall.

I would play hookey more.

I wouldn't make such good grades, except by accident.

I would ride on more merry-go-rounds.

I'd pick more daisies.[6]

TAKE ACTION

1. Learn to take five-minute vacations when stress begins to build. Find a quiet place to relax. Picture Jesus saying, **"Quiet! Be still!"** Sense your muscles relaxing and your mind calming.

2. Channel some of your stressful energy into doing something for others.

Father, thank You for understanding my stress. Bring peace to my life. Amen.

NOTES

1. Robert Frost, "The Road Not Taken," *Robert Frost's Poems* (New York: Washington Square Press, 1966), 223.

2. Leslie B. Flynn, *What Is Man?* (Wheaton, Ill.: Victor Books, 1978), 15.

3. William H. Hinson, *Solid Living in a Shattered World* (Carmel, N.Y.: Abingdon Press, 1985), 124-25.

4. Basil Miller, "Our God Is Able," in *The American Pulpit Series, Book 1* (New York: Abingdon-Cokesbury Press, 1945), 39.

5. Erling C. Olsen, *Meditations in the Book of Psalms* (Neptune, N.J.: Loizeaux Brothers, 1941 and 1967), 83.

6. Used with permission of Chariot Family Publishing, Elgin, Ill. *When I Relax I Feel Guilty,* by Tim Hansel, 1979, 44-45. Available at your local Christian bookstore.